Law 25 Wide ball. If the bowler bowls the ball and, in the opinion of the umpire, it is too wide or too high for the batsman to reach from his normal guard position the umpire shall call and ⬚⬚⬚ ⬚l a wide ball: if however the batsman leaves his guard p⬚⬚⬚⬚ ⬚⬚ ⬚⬚t the ball comes within his reach the ball is not the⬚ ⬚ wide.

Law 36 LBW (leg b⬚⬚⬚⬚ ⬚⬚⬚⬚⬚)
If the batsma⬚ ⬚⬚⬚⬚⬚ ⬚⬚ it with his bat or a hand holdin⬚ ⬚⬚⬚ ⬚⬚⬚⬚ ⬚ket with any other part of his ⬚⬚⬚⬚ ⬚⬚ ⬚⬚ out LBW if the point of impac⬚ ⬚⬚⬚ ⬚⬚⬚⬚kets and the ball did not first pitch ⬚ ⬚⬚ ⬚⬚⬚

If the batsman di⬚ ⬚⬚⬚ ⬚⬚⬚⬚⬚ ⬚⬚ play the ball he may be given out LBW even if the poi⬚ ⬚⬚⬚⬚⬚pact is outside the line of his off stump.

In both these cases the umpire will only give the batsman out if he is satisfied that the ball was going to hit the wicket if it had not been intercepted.

Fig A   Fig B

Fig 'A' The batsman cannot be given out if the ball strikes the leg which is outside the leg stump. Fig 'B' The batsman can be given out if he does not play a stroke and the ball strikes the leg which is outside the off stump.

If the batsman has played a stroke he is only out LBW if the ball was going to hit the wicket and the point of impact is within the blue shaded area.

If the batsman did not play a stroke he may be given out LBW if the ball was going to hit the wicket even though the point of impact is outside the shaded area and on the off side.

From family cricket right through to Test cricket, this book will show you how cricket should be played and many of the rules that you should know.

A booklet containing all the Laws of Cricket may be obtained from Marylebone Cricket Club (Sales Department), Lords Cricket Ground, London NW8 8QN. (Present cost 50p excluding postage.)

Acknowledgments

The author and publishers wish to thank Leicestershire County Cricket Club for their assistance, and Mr David Swift for his advice and help in the preparation and content of this book, and also for the use of the engraving on page 4. Additional photographic material on pages 17, 24, 27, 39 and 42 was provided by All-Sport Photographic Agency, and Harry Prince (Sports Outfitter) Ltd provided cricket equipment for photographing.

First edition

© LADYBIRD BOOKS LTD MCMLXXXII

Cricket

written by TONY BRADSHAW
illustrations by CHRIS REED
photographs by TIM CLARK

Ladybird Books Loughborough

Cricket has developed over a long period – five hundred years or more – from games called Stool Ball and Club Ball.

There were probably rules for cricket in existence as early as 1700, but the earliest we can be certain about date from 1744 and were used by the Artillery Club in London. In 1787, the Marylebone Cricket Club was formed, and on 30th May 1788, the first MCC code was adopted.

Ever since that date, the MCC has been the sole authority for the Laws, their interpretation and amendments.

In all the years that cricket has been played, it has always been a team game with each player trying his best, not for himself, but for his team.

The game is played not only according to the Laws of cricket but also within the spirit of the game. Because of this, it has come to be held in such high esteem that the expression 'That's not Cricket' is now widely used to refer to any act considered to be of a mean, unsporting or cheating nature.

Family cricket

Cricket isn't always the formal game played at county and international levels. Most people's introduction to the game is 'family' cricket — in the back garden or on the beach.

All you need for family cricket is a fairly level open space, a ball, a bat, a wicket of some kind, and as many enthusiastic players as you can find.

Even in cricket at this level, however, you have rules to make sure that the game is fair.

Once everyone understands what the rules are — and that they can't make them up as they go along — they will be more likely to accept and obey them.

In just the same way, the game of cricket at the highest levels is played according to a set of rules, called 'The Laws of Cricket'.

Opposite: A match at Hambledon 1777

Fielding

Everyone who wants to learn cricket wants to bat first – but since you can't play without a ball, the first things to learn are how to catch a ball, and fielding.

Start with a soft ball, and get someone to throw it gently, with an underarm action, from about a yard away. Spread your fingers, with both wrists close together. When the ball comes into your hands, your palms should touch and your fingers should close round the ball. Move both hands slightly down the line of flight that the ball was taking. (This helps to stop the ball bouncing out of your hands and being dropped.) Keep your head still, and watch the ball all the way until it is safely caught.

It will help if you are comfortably balanced on both feet, with your knees slightly bent.

As you get better, the throwing distance can be increased. When you can catch the soft ball every time, start using a cricket ball.

Taking a high catch

Up to the age of twelve, a 4¾ oz ball is best, and all the things you have learnt when catching a soft ball still apply – knees slightly bent, well balanced on both feet, head still, head and hands in line with the ball, fingers spread, hands relaxed and eyes on the ball!

Once again, start with a short distance and gradually increase it as you get better.

If you want to practise catching by yourself, throw a soft ball against a wall. This way you can experiment with high, low, hard and soft types of bounces.

A wall is also useful for a number of players to practise against. The person throwing the ball could stand behind a line of several fielders who face the wall and attempt to catch the rebound. There are many different ways of doing this and they will all help you to improve your catching.

Wall catching

A good way to practise fielding is for players to stand in a circle — three or four yards across to start with, then widening as you improve. The ball is thrown across the circle, sometimes at one height sometimes at another. The catcher soon learns to move into the line of the ball, with hands, feet, head and eyes all working together in the proper way. This cross circle throwing works quite simply with an odd number of catchers. With seven players numbered clockwise 1 throws to 4, 4 to 7, 7 to 3, 3 to 6, 6 to 2, 2 to 5, and 5 back to 1. Next time reverse the order by throwing to the person that you received from. A team that is good at catching is well on the way to becoming a winning team!

Nearly all the fielders' work however is concerned with picking up a moving ball from the ground and returning it accurately to the wicket keeper, or on certain occasions to the bowler.

When fielding, as with catching, you must position yourself correctly to stop the ball, and the *Long Barrier* position is the best way. Place yourself in the path of the ball, bend down with your hands waiting to receive the ball and your head directly over your hands. The hands should be relaxed, fingers pointing downwards with the little fingers touching. Position the heel of one foot behind your hands. The knee of your other leg should overlap the foot behind your hands. Thus your foot and leg are at right angles to the path of the ball and serve as a second line of defence should the ball make an unexpected change of direction and slip through your hands. As with

Opposite: Long barrier position

catching, you must keep your head still and watch the ball all the way into your hands.

If you can't take up the long barrier position, you should still try to gather the ball with both hands and have one foot at right angles behind your hands as a short barrier. Head and eyes must be directly over your hands and you should watch the ball all the way into your hands.

Once you've fielded the ball, you must be able to return it accurately and quickly to the wicket keeper (or sometimes to the bowler's end).

FIELDING POSITIONS

In a game of cricket, there are eleven players on each side. This means that the side which is fielding has eleven players on the field, including the bowler, while the opposing team has simply two batsmen. This diagram shows most of the important fielding positions.

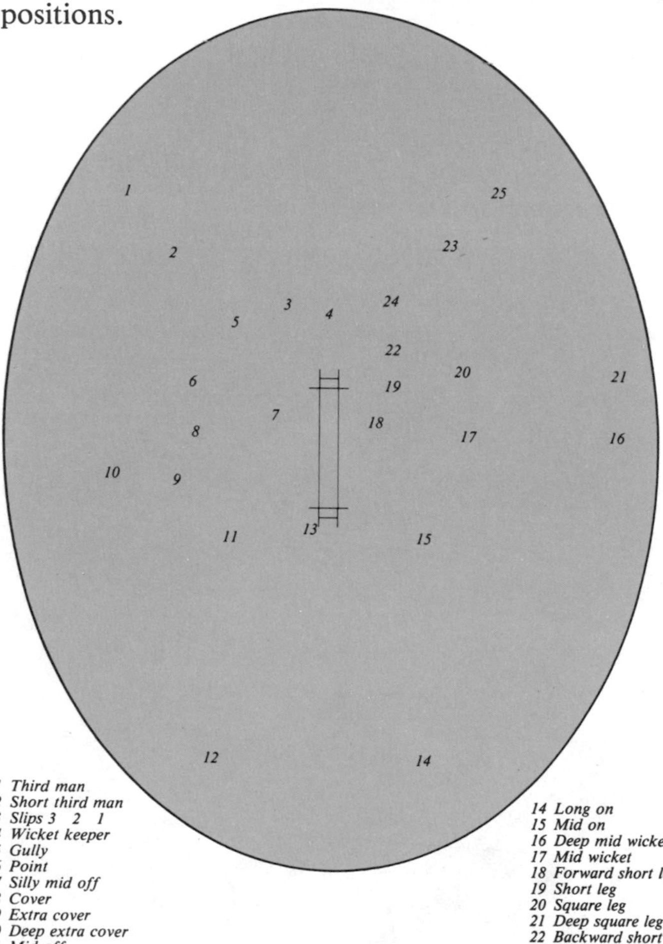

1 Third man
2 Short third man
3 Slips 3 2 1
4 Wicket keeper
5 Gully
6 Point
7 Silly mid off
8 Cover
9 Extra cover
10 Deep extra cover
11 Mid off
12 Long off
13 Bowler

14 Long on
15 Mid on
16 Deep mid wicket
17 Mid wicket
18 Forward short leg
19 Short leg
20 Square leg
21 Deep square leg
22 Backward short leg
23 Fine leg
24 Leg slip
25 Deep fine leg

*A typical field set around
the wicket for a fast bowler*

11

Fielders have to be wide awake at all times and ready to move into position to support and help the other fielders. When a batsman has struck the ball, for example towards third man, the wicket keeper should move to a position to receive the ball, with the wicket between himself and the fielder, and at the same time square leg will move to a position a short distance behind the wicket keeper in case the throw in is inaccurate.

At the other end of the pitch, the bowler will position himself by the stumps so that he can receive the ball if it is returned to him. A fielder from mid on would position himself to cover the bowler and prevent any overthrows.

As the bowler nears the end of his run up, all fielders in close catching positions should stand in a crouching position with legs apart and bent, weight evenly balanced on the balls of the feet, hands close together, but not touching, and fingers pointing downwards. The head and eyes should be still and the ball must be watched all the way from the bat.

Close fielders alert and anticipating the batsman's stroke

In junior cricket fielders should not, with the exception of the wicket keeper, stand closer than 11 yds from the middle stump at the batting end, except behind the wicket on the off side.

All fielders (other than those in close catching positions) should move towards the batsman as the ball is bowled, keeping their eyes on the ball from the moment it leaves the bowler's hand. The fielder then uses his judgement to position himself to intercept the ball and return it to the wicket keeper. He may, at his discretion, return it to the bowler's end if there is a good chance of a run out being achieved by doing this. Returning the ball quickly and accurately to the wicket keeper is very important, and much practice is needed to improve this skill and technique.

For short distances it is sometimes quicker to collect the ball and return it with an underarm throw. For longer distances, an overarm action is needed. The technique is to have the weight on the right foot, the right arm holding the ball, and the left arm pointing towards the wicket keeper. Eyes should be fixed on the wicket keeper's gloves. Transfer the weight forward along the line of the throw to the left foot, at the same time swinging the shoulders and right hand along this line, releasing the ball about halfway through, but following through fully with the throwing arm and right foot. Keep the head and the eyes looking at the target throughout the throw. With an underarm throw, you must also keep the arm swing along the intended line of travel. Watch the target throughout the throw.

Poised for the throw

The follow-through

15

Wicket keeping

The wicket keeper needs to be one of the fittest players on the field. He needs quick reflexes, a sharp eye, natural agility, complete concentration, plenty of courage and an even temperament.

There are two basic positions for a wicket keeper to stand: either close to the wicket, or standing back from the wicket. If standing close to the wicket, he should be close enough to knock the bails off, having caught the ball, without stretching too far or losing balance.

Squat with hands together, fingers pointing downwards and resting on the ground, palms open facing the bowler. The left foot should be behind middle or off stump, and the right foot a comfortable distance away with the heels off the ground and a few inches apart. The weight should be comfortably balanced between both feet and the knees should be fully bent. The head should be still and eyes level.

The wicket keeper must watch the bowler, and follow the ball all the way into his hands. He must assume that every ball bowled is going to reach him. (He should stay in the squatting position until he sees the ball strike the ground, and should rise with the ball into a crouching position in order to catch it at or about knee height.)

He must always be in a position to take any stumping chances that present themselves although his main object is always to catch the ball cleanly after every delivery.

Squat position

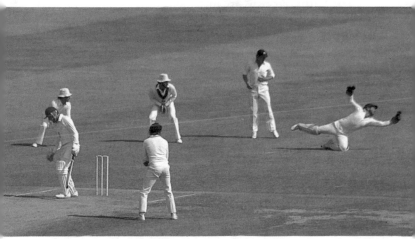

Rod Marsh (Australia) takes a leg side catch off Bill Athey (England)

Wicket keeper in crouching position

For fast bowlers he should stand back from the wicket in such a position that he is able to catch a good length delivery between knee and waist height just after it has passed the highest point of its first bounce.

He should position himself behind the wicket or just far enough to the off side to enable him to get a good and early sighting of the ball. Exactly where he stands will depend to a great deal on how the batsman positions himself. When standing back, the crouching position may be preferred to the squat. In this position, he stands with fingers facing downwards, feet comfortably apart, weight balanced between the balls of the feet, knees slightly bent and body leaning forward. Eyes should be level, head quite still over his hands, and he must get his body behind his hands in time to gather the ball cleanly. He should not however move sideways until he is certain of the correct path of the ball.

Gloves

The choice of comfortable, well fitting, flexible gloves is most important for a wicket keeper (a slightly roughened, cupped surface in the palms will help the ball to stick). Inner gloves of cotton or chamois leather should also be worn.

Pads

These are a second line of defence and should not be too large or cumbersome. Remember that the wicket keeper has to be agile and must be able to move quickly on many occasions.

Boots

These should be comfortable and stud length kept to a minimum − long studs tend to press against the feet on hard wickets, and also dig into the pitch making quick turns difficult. A comfortable pair of clean socks are a must.

An athletic protector should always be worn when playing or practising, and in sunny conditions a well fitting cap is also essential.

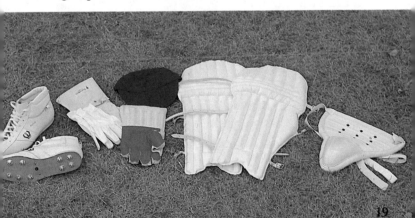

The bat

Choose your bat carefully, and make sure it is not too heavy or too big for you.

If your bat is looked after properly, it will give you good service. Don't keep it in a damp place, and follow the maker's instructions about its care and maintenance.

Batting

Concentrate fully on each ball, no matter how many runs have been made. Always try to put the bowler and fielders on the defensive – attack whenever prudent and possible.

The following applies to a right handed player, as do all instructions in this book, but by changing left for right and right for left the instructions will then apply to left handed players.

Grip

Hold the handle with the hands close together and the right hand below the left. The V made by the thumb and forefinger of the right hand should be between the centre of the rear of the bat (the splice) and the offside edge of the bat. The V made by the left hand should be directly above that of the right hand,

and the fingers and thumbs should grip the handle firmly.

Taking guard

This is to help the batsman to know exactly where his bat is in relation to the wickets. The batsman, holding his bat vertically in front of his wickets, will ask the umpire for 'centre, middle and leg', or whatever position he wishes his bat to be guarding whilst awaiting the bowler's delivery. The umpire, standing directly behind the bowler's wicket, will indicate to the batsman when his bat is guarding the wicket or wickets he has selected. The batsman may then make a mark to enable him to take up his correct position quickly for each bowling delivery. He must not make a hole in the pitch.

A batsman will, with practice, develop his own style. The following advice is intended to help new players to start their cricket without any 'built-in errors' which may take years to correct later on.

Batsman taking guard

21

Stance

Stand with your feet close together, but not touching, with one foot each side of the popping crease. Your knees should be slightly bent and the weight equally balanced on both legs and feet. Your chest should be facing point position and the left shoulder pointing down the line of the wicket to the bowler's end. Turn your head towards the bowler, and keep it still, with the eyes as level as possible. The bat should be touching the ground just behind your right toe, with the blade in a nearly vertical position facing the bowler. Your hands may be just touching your left leg above the knee.

The backlift

Before a carpenter or handyman hits a nail with a hammer, he swings the head of the hammer backwards and then strikes forward. In cricket it is equally important for a batsman to lift his bat backwards before starting forward movement. Since the wickets are upright behind the batsman the backlift should also be upright keeping the bat in line with the wickets, so that on making the forward stroke it will move through a vertical arc in front of the wickets and along the line of the ball. In this way the batsman will be giving maximum protection to his wickets, regardless of the type of stroke that he decides to play.

Batting strokes can be divided into Forward or Backward and Attacking or Defending.

The forward defensive stroke

The left leg moves forward along the line of the ball and the foot is placed close to the pitch of the ball. At the same time the head, close to the left shoulder, rather like a boxer, also moves forward along the line of the ball. As always the batsman must watch the ball all the way on to the face of his bat. The bat must be almost vertical, but the handle should be well forward of the blade so that the ball will not be hit in an upwards direction. There is no follow through in this stroke.

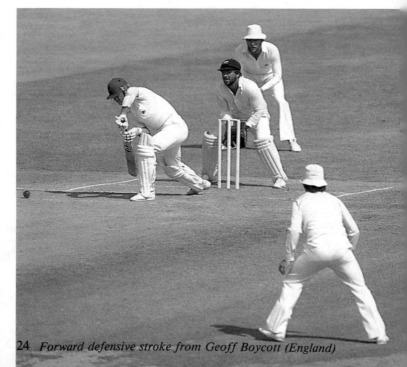

Forward defensive stroke from Geoff Boycott (England)

Playing back in defence

Sometimes it's necessary to play back, in order to have a little more time to watch the ball. To play this stroke the right leg moves backwards along the line of the ball. The head should be close to the left shoulder, which should point along the line of the ball, and the batsman must *watch the ball right on to the bat*. (The left leg will move backwards after the right leg and the left foot should finish close to the right foot with the weight balanced between the two.) The higher the ball bounces the higher it will be necessary to raise the left elbow. The bat should move down the line of the ball and the hands should be well ahead of the blade at the time of impact to make sure that the ball is directed downwards. There is no follow through in this stroke.

The off drive

Since the object of a game of cricket is to score more runs than your opponents, it is desirable for a batsman to be able to play attacking strokes to all parts of the playing area.

The 'On drive' and the 'Off drive' are both extensions of, or natural progressions from, the Forward Defensive Stroke. With both drives, the bat accelerates in an arc along the line of the ball, and follows through, completing the arc whilst the body weight is transferred on to the front foot.

ATTACKING STROKES OFF THE BACK FOOT

The pull

This is a cross batted stroke, played to a short pitched ball, that pulls the ball round to the on side.

The batsman moves his right foot back to a position just in front of his off stump, with the toe pointing towards mid off. The left leg is moved back so that the batsman is standing square to the line of the ball. The bat is pulled round, crossing the front of the batsman whose head should be above and behind the bat along the line of the ball. The pull is completed by the follow through of the bat in a horizontal position about waist high, with the right hand rolling over the left, the blade facing downwards, and the weight being transferred to the left foot.

Viv Richards (West Indies) pulls to leg

The start of the hook

The hook

This is similar to the pull, but is played to a fast, high bouncing ball below shoulder height. The batsman's footwork is similar to that for the pull, but the body pivots on the right foot, so that on completion the left leg will be closest to the wickets and the batsman will be nearly square on, facing square leg. As the ball has been played from a higher position than the pull, the bat will have completed an arc, parallel to the ground, about shoulder height. Again, to prevent the ball from being hit too high, the right hand must be rolled over the left to turn the blade as the ball is struck. The head must be kept in line with the ball, and the ball must be *watched right on to the bat*.

The finish of the hook

28

A sweep shot from Mike Brearley (England)

The sweep

This stroke can be employed against a slowish ball outside the leg stump, and sweeps the ball round in the area occupied by long leg or fine leg. The left leg will move round into the line of the ball and should be slightly bent in order to let the bat be swung round in a horizontal arc. On striking the ball the blade of the bat should 'roll' slightly over the ball to stop it being hit upwards.

The leg glance

This may be played off either the front foot or the
back foot and should only be used on a ball that is
outside the line of the leg stump. Played off the front
foot the initial action is similar to that of a forward
defensive stroke except that the bat will be in front of
the left pad. As contact is made with the ball, the
wrists are turned to deflect the ball wide of the wicket
keeper, down the leg side. The head must be over the
vertical bat and the ball should be *watched all the way
on to the blade of the bat*. There is no follow through
in this stroke.

The square cut and the late cut

The cut may be used against short pitched balls well wide of the off stump. Both strokes are played with a horizontal bat and with the arms at full stretch. The bat is moved from the high backlift and comes down on to the ball from above. The right foot is moved to a position outside the off stump, with the toe pointing in the intended direction of the stroke. For a *square cut*, the ball is struck as it reaches the popping crease, for a *late cut* it is struck as it nears the line of the stumps with the batsman facing in the direction of third man.

One of the most important things that a batsman must learn is how to run between the wickets. It is not only well hit boundaries that win matches; those batsmen who are able to recognise quickly and run the single, second and third runs when they are available are also match winners. To achieve a high standard of running, good 'calling' is essential.

The general rule on calling is that if the ball passes behind the striker, the batsman at the bowler's end should call. If the ball is in front of the striker, the striker should call.

The three single words used are:

YES — means run

NO — means do not run

WAIT — means there may be a chance of a run if the fielder is unable to intercept or gather the ball cleanly.

All calls should be loud, clear and decisive. If the non-calling batsman sees that a run would be too risky, he may refuse the call with a quick, loud NO. But this refusal must be immediate, and once a run has started there should be no hesitation and the run should be attempted no matter what happens. Always be on the lookout for the second or third run, but call clearly each time.

The batsman who is running towards the stumps which are closer to the ball is the correct person to call for a second or third run, since he is running towards the end that the fielder is most likely to throw to.

The batsman at the bowler's end should not stand still during the delivery. He should hold his bat in the hand nearest to the bowler, stand wide of the return crease and after the bowler releases the ball he should move two paces down the side of the pitch. If the call is YES, he runs down the wicket on the opposite side from that on which the bowler is bowling. The striker should run down the bowler's side. The batsmen may NOT run down the middle of the wicket because their studs are very likely to damage the playing surface.

On nearing the popping crease at the other end of the run each batsman should ground his bat in front of him and slide it along the ground. It is important to do this and ensure that the bat runs in over the popping crease. Failure to ground the bat behind the popping crease after each run will result in a 'short run' if the batsman turns for a second run.

Non striker backing up

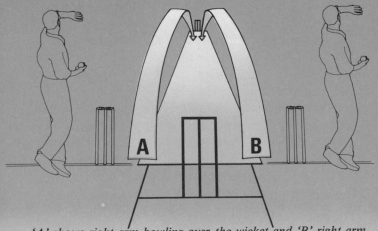

'A' shows right arm bowling over *the wicket and 'B' right arm bowling* round *the wicket*

Bowling

For a delivery to be fair, the ball must be bowled and not thrown. The ball is deemed to have been thrown if the process of straightening the bowling arm takes place during the delivery swing which directly precedes the ball leaving the hand. This means that the bowling arm must be straight throughout the delivery swing until the ball has been released, but does not prevent the use of the wrist during the delivery.

A bowler is said to be bowling 'over the wicket' if his bowling arm is closest to the wicket at the bowler's end. He is bowling 'round the wicket' if the wicket at his end is closest to his non-bowling arm.

Bowlers are usually classified according to the speed of their delivery – Fast, Medium paced or Slow. The bowlers of slower moving deliveries rely on turning the ball and varying its flight through the air.

The bowlers of fast deliveries rely largely on the speed of their bowling and variation in bounce and line.

Medium paced bowlers rely on a combination of speed, swing and spin.

In general, all bowlers should develop accuracy of length and direction, and must try to force the batsman to play at every delivery. On approaching the bowling crease, the bowler's action is rather like that of someone preparing to do a cartwheel towards the batsman. The body should be sideways on to the intended bowling line with head and eyes concentrating on the stumps at the batsman's end.

A common fault which many juniors acquire is that of taking too long a run up in an attempt to bowl fast. When learning to bowl it is best to start standing still and practise the delivery action only and to concentrate on bowling a correct line and accurate length. It is only when these skills have been mastered that increased speed should be attempted.

4   5

There are five key positions through which a bowler should pass in his delivery. In broad principle figs 1 and 2 represent the winding-up of the body into what is known as the 'coil' position, fig 4 the follow-through and fig 5 the actual bowling. Fig 3 is the half-way stage, and one to which nearly all the great bowlers have in fact conformed

Always remember that a run up should start slowly, accelerate smoothly and only reach maximum speed in time for the delivery stride.

The last two strides of a bowler's run up are the most important and consist of a jump or leap off the left foot on to the right foot. During this leap, and whilst in the air, the body and shoulders are turned sideways (so that the hands are in the 'coil' position). The right hand holding the ball should be about chin high and the left arm should be bent (with the hand near the right shoulder). Keep looking down the wicket over your left elbow. By now the arm will have straightened out and be pointing vertically upwards and the body and shoulders will be sideways on to the pitch. The left leg moves forward and the right arm should stretch fully backwards at about 180° to the left arm which comes forward and down in a vertical arc. Your eyes behind the arm should be concentrating on the stumps at the batsman's end of the pitch.

The left foot will land on or behind the popping crease and the right arm follows the left through the same arc. The ball will be released at about its highest point in the arc, which should occur about the moment the left foot touches the ground.

Throughout the run up and delivery, the bowler must concentrate on his direction line and the point at which he intends the ball to pitch. Before starting each run up, he should also have decided exactly what type of ball he is intending to bowl.

Australian fast bowler Dennis Lillee in action

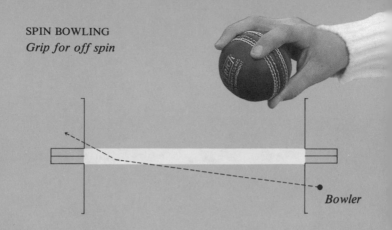

Bowler

Dotted line shows flight of ball for off spin

Off spin

The thumb, first and second fingers are all widely spaced, gripping the seam which rests also on the bent third finger. As the ball is released, the wrist is turned clockwise rather like turning a door knob and the first and second fingers pull downwards whilst the thumb moves upwards and over the top of the ball. It is the first and second fingers that give the spinning movement to the ball. On completion of the delivery swing, the right arm moves across the body with the palm of the hand uppermost. An off break is one which changes direction for a turn or break to the right after pitching and a leg break turns in the opposite direction.

Leg break

The thumb and first two fingers grip the seam of the ball but are not so widely spaced as for an off

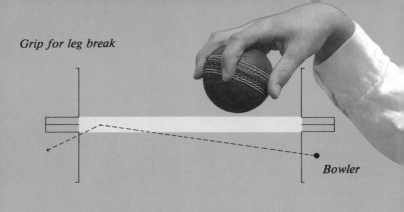

Grip for leg break

Bowler

Dotted line shows flight of ball for leg break

break. The third finger lies along the seam. The wrist is bent as far as possible at the start of the delivery swing and is straightened out as the ball is released, whilst at the same time the third and fourth fingers push upwards giving an anti-clockwise rotation to the ball.

SWING BOWLING

The ability to make a ball swing in the air is one of the arts of a fast or medium paced bowler. The amount of swing will depend very much on the weather. A heavy atmosphere and favourable wind direction coupled with a new ball are considered ideal for a swing bowler.

The theory, in brief, is that the shiny side of the ball will offer less resistance to the air, and the rough side will offer greater resistance and will travel more slowly. The ball will thus turn towards the rough side. The wind will also help to push the ball out of its original line of flight.

41

Outswing

If the wind is blowing towards the bowler but from the leg side, this will favour the outswing bowler. The first and second fingers are on each side of the seam but slightly across it, the thumb is on the bottom of the seam, the shiny side of the ball is on the side of the third and fourth fingers. The seam is pointed in the direction of first slip at the moment of delivery. For outswing, the bowler should exaggerate the

Ian Botham (England) expert in the use of the swing ball

shoulder rotation during the 'bound'. In delivery the wrist should be a little stiffer than normal and the two fingers should remain in contact with the ball as long as possible in order to give back spin to the ball.

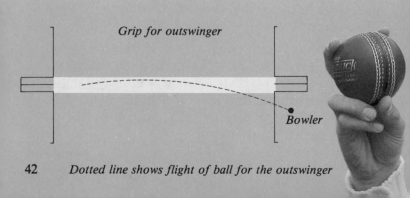

Grip for outswinger

Bowler

Dotted line shows flight of ball for the outswinger

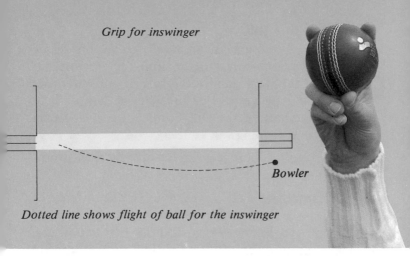

Grip for inswinger

Bowler

Dotted line shows flight of ball for the inswinger

Inswing

If the wind is blowing towards the bowler but from the off side, this will favour the inswing bowler. The first and second fingers are on each side of the seam, and the seam itself is angled slightly in the direction of fine leg. The rough side of the ball is on the side of the third and fourth fingers. For inswing, the bowler should be slightly more square on to the batsman than normal. The bowler's left shoulder will point towards slip rather than down the wicket. As for outswing, the two fingers should remain in contact with the ball as long as possible to give back spin.

The bowler has, in each case, applied back spin to the ball. The seam should rotate rather like an equator as the ball travels through the air. The rotation of the seam should be in a vertical plane but slightly across the line of flight towards the direction of intended swing.

The captain's job

A good captain may mean the difference between a team winning or losing a match, and it is very difficult to find all the ideal qualities in one person! In order to command the respect of his side, he will need to be good at batting, bowling (unless he is a wicket keeper), and fielding.

The captain should always be smartly turned out, and should insist that his team is also.

The captain needs to have a complete knowledge of the rules of the game. He must also be a good tactician, and know the capabilities of his bowlers, batsmen and fielders. When fielding, he should be in a position from where he can signal to any player to indicate field adjustments. He also needs to be where he can easily communicate with his bowlers: mid on or mid off are two suitable positions. (This should be done in a quiet manner without a lot of shouting and arm waving.)

Captains spinning up

The captain must be prepared to alter his bowling or batting order if he deems it necessary, but should avoid too many changes since they might upset the balance of the team. He should always resist any pressure applied by the opposing team or their supporters to make an unwise declaration which may lose his team the match. The captain's job is rather like that of a military commander: he has to use the forces under his command in order to win the match, and if that becomes impossible, he has to mount a 'rearguard action' to ensure that he does not lose it.

The umpires

Two umpires are appointed to control the game and to apply the Laws with complete impartiality.

During play one umpire stands behind the stumps at the bowler's end and the other umpire will generally stand on the leg side of the striker, square on to the wicket. Both umpires must position themselves so that they are best able to see any act or acts upon which they may be required to make a decision and should stand where they do not interfere with the bowler's run up or the striker's view.

There are nine recognised signals which are used by the umpires to communicate to the scorers such things as boundaries, byes, leg byes, no balls, short runs and wides.

The umpires are the sole judges of fair and unfair play and they alone determine and settle all disputes that may arise.

Six-a-side

You do not have to play cricket with 22 players. Six-a-side cricket can be great fun, and you can play a whole match in an hour! You need six people on each team, and here is how it's played.

1 Each fielding side bowls ten overs, with each player (except the wicket keeper) bowling two.

2 When batting, as soon as any batsman reaches or passes an agreed score (say 25), he must retire.

3 If five wickets fall before the ten overs are completed, the last batsman plays on, receiving all deliveries, with the other batsman acting as a

runner from the other end. If either batsman or runner are out, the innings is over.

4 The team scoring the most runs in its innings is the winner. If both teams score the same number of runs, the team which lost fewest wickets is the winner. If still equal, the result may be decided on a 'bowling at the wicket' trial. This means that five members of each team bowl one ball at the stumps. (First a member of one team, then a member of the other team, and so on.) The team which hits the stumps most times is the winner. (This is rather like a drawn football match being decided on penalties.)

First class cricket

There has been a trend in recent years for first class cricketers to play 'one day' or 'limited over' cricket in addition to the normal three-day matches. This shortened form of cricket is often played on Sundays, the whole single innings match is completed in one day and they frequently provide some very close and exciting results.

Since the emphasis has to be on attacking strokes, because of the limited number of overs available for the batsmen to score runs, the games are more likely to produce exciting cricket to watch. Equally, the defending side by its keen fielding can create excitement in the contest to prevent runs being scored.

40 over matches

In this game the fielding sides bowl a total of only 40 overs (less if they bowl out their opponents before they complete 40 overs). No bowler is permitted to bowl more than 8 overs, so a minimum of 5 bowlers is used.

An interesting feature of this game is that the side batting second knows exactly how many runs they require to win, and how many overs are available to them, to achieve their target. The second innings becomes a matter of the number of runs per over needed and, as each over passes, interest centres on whether the 'scoring rate' is being achieved. (Keeping up with or ahead of the scoring rate is important because if the game has to be stopped due to bad weather, before a conclusion has been reached, then the team with the superior scoring rate is adjudged the winner.)

55 and 60 over matches

These are similar to the above except that each bowler is limited to 11 or 12 overs and each innings will last about an hour more.

A typical limited-overs stroke from Roland Butcher (England)

The County Championship is decided on a league basis. A match consists of two innings by each team. The matches are of three days' duration and, at the present time, points are awarded to the teams as follows:

a 16 points for a win, plus any points gained on the first innings.

b 8 points for each side in a tie, plus any first innings points.

c If the scores are equal in a drawn match, the side batting in the fourth innings scores 8 points, plus any points scored in the first innings.

d First innings points are awarded only for performances in the first 100 overs of each first innings as follows:

(i) Batting points: 150-199 runs = 1 point
200-249 runs = 2 points
250-299 runs = 3 points
300 or more runs = 4 points

The maximum number of batting points available is 4.

(ii) Bowling points: 3-4 wickets taken = 1 point
5-6 wickets taken = 2 points
7-8 wickets taken = 3 points
9-10 wickets taken = 4 points

e If less than eight hours' playing time remains, a one innings match may be played. In this case no first innings points are awarded and the side winning the one innings match scores 12 points.

f The side with the highest aggregate of points at the end of the season becomes the Champion County. If two or more sides are equal on points, then the side with the greatest number of wins will be the champions.

The total hours of play over three days, excluding intervals, will be not less than 19 hours.

Test Matches are rather similar to County Championship Matches with the following major differences:

a Test Matches are played between countries. Australia, England, India, Pakistan, New Zealand, Sri Lanka, and West Indies are the present 'Test' playing countries.

b The duration of the match is usually five playing days but this may be reduced to three days in some cases.

c There is no restriction on the number of overs to be bowled in either of the first two innings.

d A Test Series usually consists of 5 separate matches and the team that wins the highest number of matches is said to have won the series but the number of matches played may vary.

Grandstand view at Trent Bridge, Nottingham, one of England's Test-playing grounds

INDEX